The Dame of Faketown

Level 8 – Purple

Helpful Hints for Reading at Home

The graphemes (written letters) and phonemes (units of sound) used throughout this series are aligned with Letters and Sounds. This offers a consistent approach to learning whether reading at home or in the classroom. Books levelled as 'a' are an introduction to this band. Readers can advance to 'b' where graphemes are consolidated and further graphemes are introduced.

HERE IS A LIST OF ALTERNATIVE GRAPHEMES FOR THIS PHASE OF LEARNING. AN EXAMPLE OF THE PRONUNCIATION CAN BE FOUND IN BRACKETS.

Phase 5 Alternative Pronunciations of Graphemes			
a (hat, what)	e (bed, she)	i (fin, find)	o (hot, so)
u (but, unit)	c (cat, cent)	g (got, giant)	ow (cow, blow)
ie (tied, field)	ea (eat, bread)	er (farmer, herb)	ch (chin, school, chef)
y (yes, by, very)	ou (out, shoulder, could, you)		
o_e (home)	u_e (rule)		

HERE ARE SOME WORDS WHICH YOUR CHILD MAY FIND TRICKY.

Phase 5 Tricky Words			
oh	their	people	Mr
Mrs	looked	called	asked
could			

TOP TIPS FOR HELPING YOUR CHILD TO READ:

• Allow children time to break down unfamiliar words into units of sound and then encourage children to string these sounds together to create the word.

• Encourage your child to point out any focus phonics when they are used.

• Read through the book more than once to grow confidence.

• Ask simple questions about the text to assess understanding.

• Encourage children to use illustrations as prompts.

This book is an 'a' level and is a purple level 8 book band.

The Dame of Faketown

Illustrated by
Simona Hodonova

Written by
John Wood

The Dame of Faketown was fed up. People were walking outside. They were joyful. It was another boring day.

"What is wrong, Dame?" asked the cleaner.

The Dame had an idea. She felt strange. Then she felt excited. She jumped up. "No one is allowed to walk on the ground!" she said.

The Dame ran out of the room, shouting all the way. This was a good idea. This might be her best idea ever. Even better than the Big Homework Fire.

The Dame of Faketown ran to the roof. All the people below looked up at her. She beamed. "From now on, no one is allowed to walk on the ground!" she yelled.

The townspeople were scared. Their eyes were wide. They didn't know what to do.
"No way!"
"Is that safe?"

"This is not good at all!"
"You can't stop us doing that."
"Are you insane?"
"Where did you learn to be a dame?"

But the Dame of Faketown did not hear them. She jumped into her plane and flew into the air.

"And if you do go on the ground, I will send you to prison for a hundred years!"

The townspeople all looked for a place to go. The baker climbed a tree. The postwoman sat on her van. The teacher didn't know where to go, so she sat on the fence.

"Quick! Let's go to the playground," said the children. They climbed on the swings. They climbed on the monkey bars.

They climbed on the seesaw. They climbed on the roundabout. There was no time to waste. They climbed on the slide, but that was a bad idea!

"This is stupid!" said the headmaster, swinging from a rope.
"Very stupid," said the zookeeper, hanging on to a bird. "Someone needs to say something to the Dame and put a stop to this."

"My cakes are burning. I blame the Dame!" said the cakemaker.
"That shop is burning. I blame the Dame!" said the firefighter.

Just then, a hot air balloon rose into the air. The teacher was inside. She was going to get the Dame.

"I'm coming too," shouted the headmaster. The headmaster did a big swing on the rope. He flew high in the air and reached out for the hot air balloon.

The headmaster missed the hot air balloon. He didn't even get close. He fell a long, long way down.

"It's all right," said the headmaster. "I've landed in a tree. I didn't go on the ground!" The teacher waved to the red-faced headmaster. The wind whisked the balloon into the sunset.

The balloon chased the plane past the clouds and the stars.
"Please, stop all of this," said the teacher.
"This is no way for a dame to behave."

"Never!" yelled the Dame.
But then there was a scream from below. They looked down.

It was the baker. He was at the top of a tall tree and it was swaying in the wind. It looked like it was going to snap.

"I will save you!" said the Dame of Faketown. The plane dived. It chugged and chattered as it went faster and faster.

The tree was swaying even more. The baker screamed. The teacher did not know how to make a hot air balloon go downwards. Everyone gasped. Was the Dame too late?

The plane swooped down, and the Dame caught the baker as he fell out of the tree. She was just in time!

They landed, safe and sound on the ground. Everyone cheered. The baker was dazed, but he was glad to be out of the tree.
"What a day," said the postwoman. "Maybe we can go back on the ground now. What do you say?"

The Dame nodded.
"Yes, I think that sounds perfect," she said.

The next day, people's feet were planted to the floor, safe and sound. They were all joyful. It was all back to the way it was.

But the Dame of Faketown was fed up again. She tapped her fingers. She stamped her feet. Then, she smiled. She was thinking of a new idea.
The cleaner shook his head.
"I'm moving to another town," he said.

The Dame of Faketown

1. What is the Dame's best idea ever?

2. Where did the children go?
   (a) The playground
   (b) Home
   (c) The shops

3. Who did the Dame save from the top of a tall tree?

4. How do the people of Faketown feel about the Dame?

5. What would you have done if you lived in Faketown?
   Do you think you would like to live in Faketown?

©2020 **BookLife Publishing Ltd.**
King's Lynn, Norfolk PE30 4LS

ISBN 978-1-83927-312-4

All rights reserved. Printed in Malaysia.
A catalogue record for this book is available from the British Library.

The Dame of Faketown
Written by John Wood
Illustrated by Simona Hodonova

An Introduction to BookLife Readers...

Our Readers have been specifically created in line with the London Institute of Education's approach to book banding and are phonetically decodable and ordered to support each phase of the Letters and Sounds document.

Each book has been created to provide the best possible reading and learning experience. Our aim is to share our love of books with children, providing both emerging readers and prolific page-turners with beautiful books that are guaranteed to provoke interest and learning, regardless of ability.

BOOK BAND GRADED using the Institute of Education's approach to levelling.

PHONETICALLY DECODABLE supporting each phase of Letters and Sounds.

EXERCISES AND QUESTIONS to offer reinforcement and to ascertain comprehension.

BEAUTIFULLY ILLUSTRATED to inspire and provoke engagement, providing a variety of styles for the reader to enjoy whilst reading through the series.

AUTHOR INSIGHT:
JOHN WOOD

An incredibly creative and talented author, John Wood has written about 60 books for BookLife Publishing. Born in Warwickshire, he graduated with a BA in English Literature and English Language from De Montford University. During his studies, he learned about literature, styles of language, linguistic relativism, and psycholinguistics, which is the study of the effects of language on the brain. Thanks to his learnings, John successfully uses words that captivate and resonate with children and that will be sure to make them retain information. His stories are entertaining, memorable, and extremely fun to read.

This book is an 'a' level and is a purple level 8 book band.